# Small Things Lil Peter Make A BIG Difference

### BY PETER VALDEZ AND TASCHE LAINE
### ILLUSTRATED BY MEI MEI LEONARD

SKYE BLUE PRESS

This book is a work of fiction. Any references to historical events, real people, or real places are used fictitiously. Other names, characters, places, and events are products of the author's imagination, and any resemblance to actual events, organizations, locales, or persons, living or dead, is entirely coincidental.

SMALL THINGS LIL PETER MAKE A BIG DIFFERENCE. Copyright © 2022 by Tasche Laine and Peter Valdez III. All rights reserved.

Copyright fuels creativity, promotes free speech, and creates a vibrant culture. Thank you for buying an authorized edition of this book and for complying with copyright laws by not reproducing, scanning, or distributing any part of it in any form without permission. You are supporting writers and allowing Skye Blue Press to continue to publish books for readers everywhere.

Library of Congress Control Number: 2022909015
Printed in the United States of America
First Edition 2022

ISBN-13: 978-1-955674-28-7 (hardcover)
ISBN-13: 978-1-955674-29-4 (paperback)
ISBN-13: 978-1-955674-30-0 (ebook)

Skye Blue Press
Vancouver, WA
https://skyebluepress.com

*For Bridget and Jas*

*Two paws up to my sister Bridget,
who volunteers with
Northwest German Shepherd Rescue
(northwestgermanshepherd.org)
my good friend Jas List,
who runs OC Pom Rescue
(ocpomrescue.com)*

*and all the volunteers
who make a difference daily,
working hard to find good homes
for pets everywhere!
Save a life, adopt a pet today!*

—Tasche & Peter

Find more information about pet rescue in the back of this book, along with a fun, printable word search!

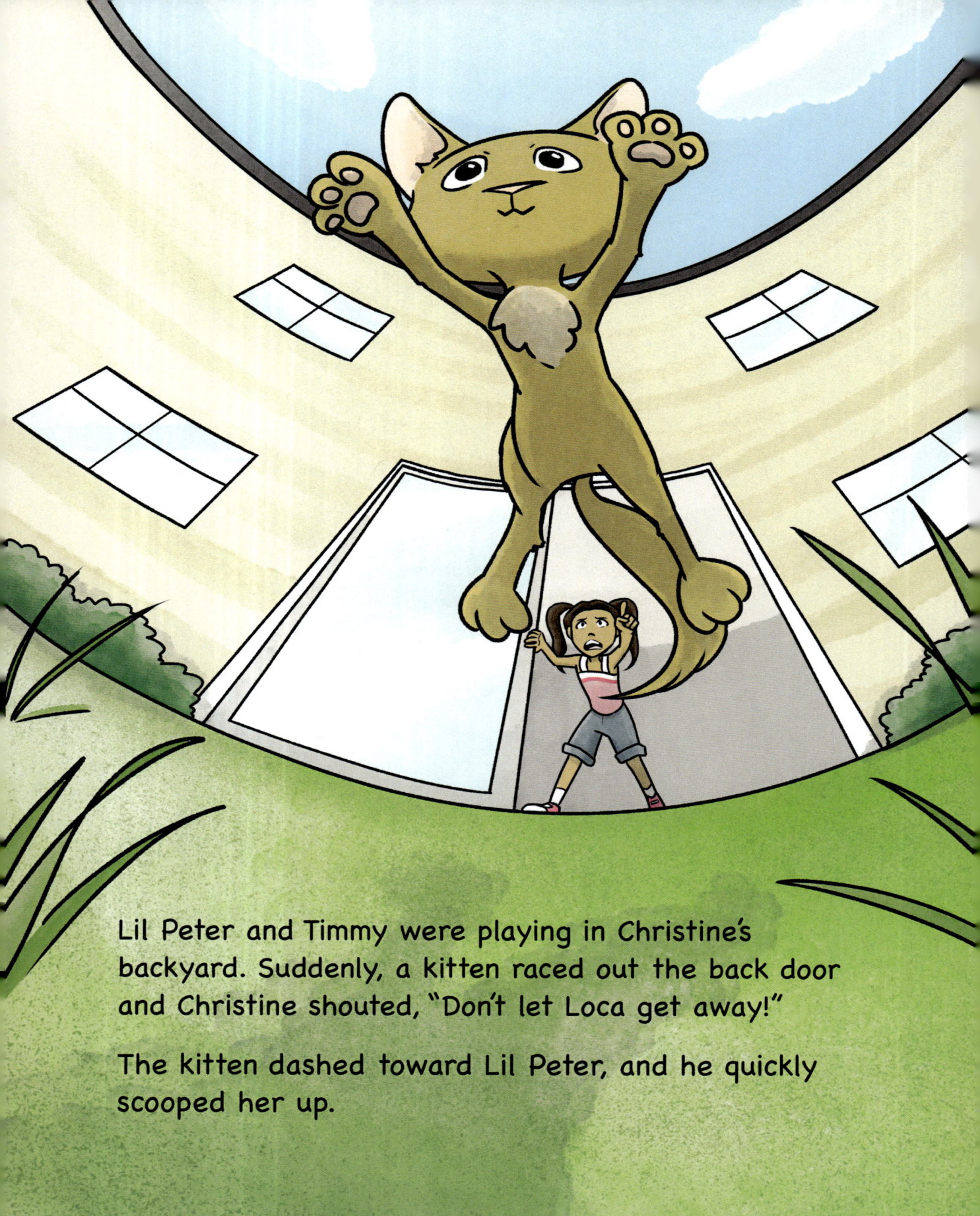

Lil Peter and Timmy were playing in Christine's backyard. Suddenly, a kitten raced out the back door and Christine shouted, "Don't let Loca get away!"

The kitten dashed toward Lil Peter, and he quickly scooped her up.

"I got her!" he said. "I didn't know you had a cat, Christine."

"I don't. I mean, she's still a kitten, and we're not keeping her. We're fostering her. I call her Loca because she's so full of energy!" Christine said as she took the kitten from Lil Peter.

"Loca is a funny name for a kitten, but what does fostering mean?" Timmy asked.

"My family works with a local pet rescue to provide special care to homeless animals, so they don't have to live in shelters," Christine said. "They stay in foster homes until they are ready to be adopted into their fur-ever homes."

"Fur-ever? You mean FORever, right?" Timmy asked.

"Nope. Since they have fur, I say fur-ever!" Christine said with a giggle. "We give them lots of cuddles and attention, and we get to make a difference by taking care of them."

"I want to help make a difference!" Lil Peter exclaimed. "Could I foster a kitten, too? Or maybe a puppy?"

"Sure, anyone can make a difference!" Christine said. "My mom says small things make a big difference. You start with a small action, and before you know it, you've done something big! But you better ask your mom first."

"I guess," Lil Peter said with a sigh, but he was no less determined.

Lil Peter rushed home to find his mom making dinner. "Mom! Christine is a foster and has a small Loca to make a big difference. I mean, can I foster a puppy? Pleeeease!"

"Slow down, Lil Peter," Mom said. "What's this about a puppy? You know, taking care of a puppy is a big responsibility. I'm not sure you're ready for that. Where did you get this idea?"

"From Christine, her family is taking care of a kitten named Loca. They volunteer at a pet rescue."

"A pet rescue, huh? Are you sure about this, Lil Peter?"

"Yes, I'm sure!" Lil Peter said, nodding. "I want to rescue a puppy!"

Suddenly, Marty jumped up!
"A puppy? Yes! Let's rescue a puppy!"

Mom smiled at her two boys and said, "First, let me call Christine's mom and see what this is all about."

After dinner, Mom called Christine's mom and got the details. They arranged for Lil Peter to volunteer at the rescue center on Saturdays. He could walk dogs and clean cages until soccer started up again. He would learn how much work goes into taking care of a puppy.

Lil Peter was excited when he heard the news. He couldn't wait to start! "This is going to be fun and easy!" he said to himself.

Lil Peter had no idea it would be so much work. Sometimes the big dogs would take him for a walk!

"Ew! My nose!" Lil Peter's eyes watered. "There are some things you just can't un-smell!"

Working at the rescue wasn't as much fun as he thought it would be. If it wasn't one thing, it was another.

"Not again!" Lil Peter cried out as the dogs jumped up on him, spilling the food. Now his clothes were dirty and smelly. He sure didn't feel like he was making a difference.

Frustrated, he wiped the gunk off his clothes. Then he looked down at a hungry dog and remembered what Christine said . . . how making a difference starts with something small.

"Hey small guy, I guess without this place you wouldn't have anything to eat, or even a chance to find a good home, huh?" Lil Peter said to the pup.

Week after week, Lil Peter worked hard to keep the pens and dogs extra clean for the visiting families. He wanted to give each dog the best chance of getting a fur-ever family.

Lil Peter did many small things without knowing what a big difference he was making to everyone around him.

Each Saturday grew more fun than the last, and soon the final Saturday at the rescue had arrived. It was busier than normal, with lots to do, and time flew.

Near the end of his day, four tiny puppies were brought into the shelter. They'd been left in a box on the side of the road. They were dirty and hungry.

Lil Peter was asked to take the puppies to a pet pen and brush them down. "That tickles!" he said as the puppies licked his face.

Christine walked in with a bowl of food. "I see you're working hard, as usual," she teased.

"Of course I am," Lil Peter teased back. "These little guys are full of licks and wiggles! It should be easy to find them a fur-ever family."

Laughing at Lil Peter, Christine said, "My mom said I get to keep Loca! Do you think your parents will let you foster one of these guys?"

Lil Peter sighed. "I'm happy you get to keep Loca, but I don't think my parents will let me foster a puppy yet. They still think it's too big of a responsibility for me."

"Are you sure about that, Lil Peter?" a voice chimed in. "Maybe you should ask them first."

Lil Peter looked up and saw his mom standing outside the pen.

"Mom!" Lil Peter exclaimed, "What are you doing here?"

"Christine's mom called me when the puppies came in," Mom said. "She told me about all the small things you have done here to make a big difference for the animals, and the families who adopt them."

"We're so proud of you, Lil Peter! Your dad and I think you are ready to foster a puppy . . . if you still want to."

"Boy, do I!" Lil Peter exclaimed, reaching down to pick up the smallest puppy. "This one! I want to foster this puppy!"

"He's so tiny, Lil Peter. Are you sure?" Christine asked.

"I'm sure!" Lil Peter said.

"Wonderful!" Mom said, smiling. "Let's get some supplies and get that puppy home."

In no time at all, Lil Peter and Marty helped Mom set up the puppy pen and dog bed.

"What will you call him, Lil Peter?" Mom asked.

"I'm going to name him Hero!" Lil Peter declared.

"That's why I picked him, because he's the smallest," Lil Peter said. "Small things can make a big difference. Hero may be small now, but someday he's going to be big, and I want to help him make a big difference with his fur-ever family!"

"That sounds wonderful!" Mom said. "It sure would be something to see first-hand. Wouldn't it be great to see three small guys making a big difference . . . together?"

Lil Peter looked at Hero. "That would be cool to see. But what do you mean, three small guys?"

Just then, Lil Peter's dad walked in. "That would be Marty, Hero, and you, Lil Peter, make three!" he said.

Marty jumped up, shouting, "WE GET TO KEEP HERO!"

Lil Peter's eyes widened as his smile stretched across his face. "You hear that, small guy? We're going to make a big difference . . . together!"

Lil Peter hugged Hero close as Hero licked his cheek. "Wow! Small things really can make a big difference. You're my Hero!"

# Not quite The End

Turn the page for more fun!

Do you want to foster a pet?

Fostering means you temporarily open your home to a rescue *dog in need until they find their own forever home. It could be for a week or a few months. While fostering, you learn all about a dog's personality, needs, habits, and quirks. Fosters also help with potty, crate, and leash training when necessary, as well as socialization.

Sometimes the history of the dogs in rescues is unknown, so please be open-minded and patient. Rescues take dog-owning experience and individual household dynamics into consideration when pairing foster homes with dogs. Most rescues provide basic supplies when they have adequate donations.

The more fosters a rescue has, the more pets they can save!

Contact a local rescue organization in your area
and save a life today!

*There are rescues for all kinds of pets!

www.ocpomrescue.com

OC Pom Rescue is a 501(c)(3) nonprofit Pomeranian rescue based in Southern California.

- Rescues Pomeranians of all ages, sizes, and conditions.
- Welcomes other small dog breeds.
- Prioritizes medical vetting and decompression time, rehabilitating and healing dogs from past traumas.
- Makes dog adoption process transparent & positive.
- Educates public about responsible dog ownership.
- Founders have 10+ years of dog rescue experience & welcome new volunteers.
- Fully foster-based in loving homes.
- Accepts donations.

www.northwestgermanshepherd.org

Northwest German Shepherd Rescue is an all-volunteer 501(c)(3) nonprofit organization based in Washington state. The rescue serves German Shepherds in need. Our network of devoted foster families provides a safe haven to German Shepherds as they make their way to quality, loving homes of their own. All adoption fees are used to cover spay/neuter procedures, shots, worming, microchips, emergency boarding, food, medications, and other surgeries as needed for adoptable dogs. We are run solely on adoption fees and donations.

| D | I | F | F | E | R | E | N | C | E | C | E |
|---|---|---|---|---|---|---|---|---|---|---|---|
| A | B | O | W | L | S | E | R | H | A | L | R |
| D | U | S | T | Y | C | A | R | R | Y | E | O |
| S | A | T | L | I | C | K | S | I | W | A | M |
| P | E | E | M | O | M | O | S | S | Y | N | A |
| P | U | R | L | T | O | G | E | T | H | E | R |
| R | I | P | E | I | A | K | Y | I | K | R | T |
| F | E | T | P | W | L | M | O | N | E | Y | Y |
| F | K | H | P | Y | M | P | U | E | K | E | Y |
| D | U | I | E | I | S | G | E | R | A | M | W |
| D | O | N | T | R | I | M | E | T | M | D | I |
| B | I | G | A | T | O | V | A | I | E | I | G |
| R | E | S | C | U | E | A | T | L | A | R | G |
| O | P | U | R | R | S | N | M | A | L | T | L |
| V | O | L | U | N | T | E | E | R | I | Y | E |
| R | U | F | C | U | D | D | L | E | S | L | S |

| | | | | | |
|---|---|---|---|---|---|
| BIG | DIRTY | KEY | MOM | RIPE | VOLUNTEER |
| BOWLS | DOG | KITTEN | MONEY | ROAM | WAGS |
| CARRY | DUSTY | LICKS | MORE | SAT | WIGGLES |
| CAT | FIRM | LILPETER | MOSSY | SMALL | |
| CHRISTINE | FOSTER | LOCA | PET | TAIL | |
| CLEANER | FUN | LOOK | PUPPY | THINGS | |
| CUDDLES | FUREVER | MAKE | PURRS | TIMMY | |
| DAD | GUNK | MARTY | RESCUE | TOGETHER | |
| DIFFERENCE | HERO | MICE | RIPE | TRIM | |

# PICTURE FIND

The objects below are scattered throughout this story.

How many can you find?

Want to read more about Lil Peter's adventures? Check out the series . . . in English and Español!

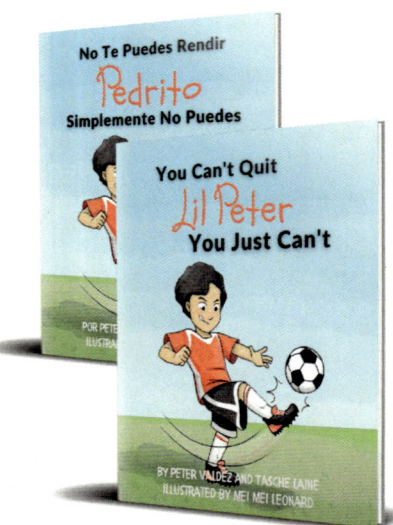

# Meet the gang

Hi there!

We hope you enjoyed our story. We strive to help children learn values while having fun.

A bit about us:
Peter & Tasche put the words on the page, Mei Mei breathes life into them with her stunning illustrations, and our newest member, Story, is the real life puppy behind Hero.

To learn more about us, please visit our website at lilpeterbooks.com.

If you enjoyed this book, please post a review at your favorite bookseller and Goodreads. Reviews help more people to find our books.

Thank you for your support!

Peter, Tasche, Mei Mei & Story

Made in the USA
Middletown, DE
22 June 2022